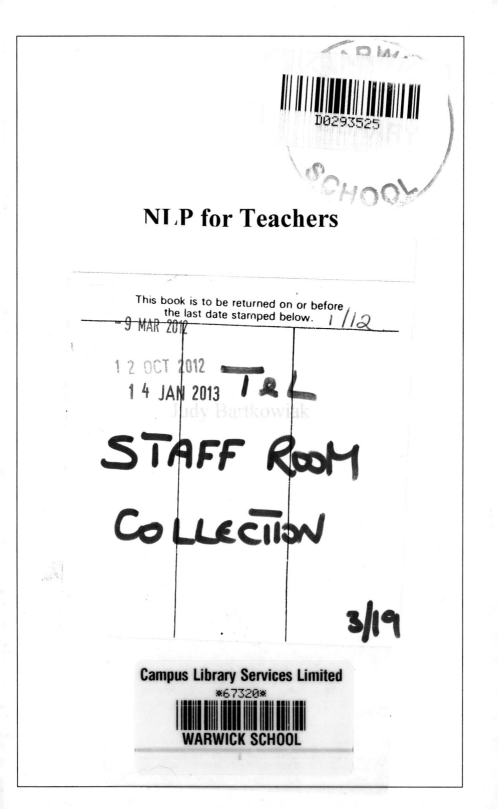

D0293525

NLP for Teachers

This book is to be returned on or before
the last date stamped below. 1/12

- 9 MAR 2012

1 2 OCT 2012   T&L
1 4 JAN 2013

STAFF ROOM

COLLECTION

3/19

Judy Bartkowiak

Campus Library Services Limited
✳67320✳

WARWICK SCHOOL

First edition published in 2010
© Copyright 2010
Judy Bartkowiak

The right of Judy Bartkowiak to be identified as the author of
this work has been asserted by her in accordance with the
Copyright, Designs and Patents Act 1998.

All rights reserved. No reproduction, copy or transmission of
this publication may be made without express prior written
permission. No paragraph of this publication may be
reproduced, copied or transmitted except with express prior
written permission or in accordance with the provisions of the
Copyright Act 1956 (as amended). Any person who commits
any unauthorised act in relation to this publication may be liable
to criminal prosecution and civil claims for damage.

Although every effort has been made to ensure the accuracy of
the information contained in this book, as of the date of
publication, nothing herein should be construed as giving
advice. The opinions expressed herein are those of the author
and not of MX Publishing.

Paperback ISBN 978-1-907685-49-1
ePub ISBN 978-1-907685-50-7
Mobipocket/Kindle ISBN 978-1-907685-51-4
Published in the UK by MX Publishing
335 Princess Park Manor, Royal Drive, London, N11 3GX
www.mxpublishing.co.uk

Cover design by www.staunch.com

ABOUT THE AUTHOR

Judy Bartkowiak is an NLP (Neuro Linguistic Programming) Master Practitioner with specialised training in working with children. She is also a qualified Personal and Pastoral Counsellor.

She is passionate about introducing NLP to kids both directly or by teaching it to parents. She runs a therapy practice working with parents, teachers, children and teens. Although she is based in the UK she also offers consultation across the world via Skype and telephone.

She says, "Over the years I have observed a wide range of teaching styles and met hundreds of teachers either through my own children or professionally running teacher workshops. This workbook covers what I feel are the most useful aspects of NLP for teachers. I feel they are life changing concepts.

I am really passionate about NLP for kids. Ever since I was first introduced to NLP by Sue Knight, (author of NLP at Work and an NLP Trainer), I have been guided by NLP principles as a parent and found them to bring about truly remarkable results."

Before her four children started school, Judy ran a Montessori Nursery School for 7 years and became aware of just how differently children learn and communicate.

Judy then returned to her career as a Market Research Consultant and used her understanding and enjoyment of working with children to specialise in children's products and TV shows. She ran hundreds of focus groups over the next 15 years with parents and children of all ages advising companies on what kids like.

She qualified in Neuro Linguistic Programming in 2001-2004 and made a career change which led Judy to taking Open University qualifications in Creative Writing. She then embarked on a writing career which has included writing children's books, copywriting and writing NLP books.

If you'd like to ask Judy about your teaching issue, be trained in NLP or arrange a workshop at your school, email her at judy@engagingnlp.com.

ENGAGING NLP

Neuro Linguistic Programming is a way of life, a new and different, positive approach to the way we communicate and how we interpret the way others communicate with us both verbally and non-verbally.

The only way to make effective changes in our life is to engage with this new way and incorporate it daily into everything we do.

At home, at work or at play, whether we are a child, a teenager or an adult, we can make new choices about how we live our life so that we achieve all we wish for in our friendships, relationships and our own state of well-being and happiness.

Engage with NLP and see, hear and feel the difference immediately.

CONTENTS

INTRODUCTION

NLP is a completely different way of viewing your world. Once you have been introduced to the NLP way of thinking and communicating it will seem like you've come home. It is respectful of others and more importantly of yourself and it is positive.

John Grinder and Richard Bandler developed what they came to call NLP from a combination of Virginia Satir's Family Therapy, Franz Perls' Gestalt Therapy and the work of Milton Erickson in the area of language patterns. What Grinder and Bandler added was the idea of coding excellence by observing how effective people communicated and forming ground rules that would bring these results to anyone who applied them. These ground rules and the tools and techniques we use to apply them are what we call NLP or Neuro Linguistic Programming.

This workbook is designed first and foremost to be a practical workbook for you to use, write in and apply on a day to day basis.

For a more in-depth read about using NLP , I have written a book in the Teach Yourself series entitled 'Be a happier parent with NLP' published by Hodder Education, which provides plenty of detail, case studies and examples.

NLP workbooks available in the *Engaging NLP* series are:

NLP for Children

NLP for Teens

NLP for Parents

NLP for Teachers

NLP Back to Work

NLP Sport

NLP Exercise and Fitness

NLP Pregnancy and Birth

NLP Setting up your own business

NLP Getting a job

THE GROUND RULES

NLP has a number of ground rules or principles that form the basis for all the practical tools and techniques you will learn in this book.

I find that they underpin it in such a way that if I get stuck, just by applying one of these rules I can find a solution. Each one makes you stop and think differently. It challenges you to assess whether what you do now, works or if by changing it, you could get a better outcome.

NLP is completely focussed on positivity, aiming for a positive outcome, a compelling outcome that is desirable for you. The focus is on what you want, rather than what you don't want.

There are even some toxic words that by avoiding will steer you a positive, resourceful path.

NLP uses a great deal too much jargon in my opinion and so I have reworded some of the concepts to make them more digestible as you will want to pass them on to your class.

1)   If you always do what you've always done
then you will always get what you've always got

This phrase had an amazing impact on me when I first heard it. Suddenly I realised that I could influence the results I got and that I had some control over what happened in my life.

Say it over to yourself slowly – "If I always do what I've always done then I will always get what I've always got."

What it means is that if you don't like 'what you've always got' you can change what you do and get something different, better. You can get better results by doing something else.

Now if you're perfectly happy with the results you're getting in the classroom and at home with your family then that's great. This phrase simply serves as a reminder then that what you are doing is working to give you the results you want. That may be enough for you.

However, if you think that you could get better results –
and by that I don't just mean academically but also in
terms of engagement with the lesson, attendance, quality
of participation and so on – then think about what you
could do differently in order to get a different result.

You can't make children listen, make them engage or
make them want to learn in fact although you can ask
children to do something, you can't make them. So if you
want to change their behaviour and that includes attitude
and language patterns, you need to change your own.

We do what we do (our behaviour) because of the beliefs
we have about that behaviour. How we do it, our skills, are
also based on beliefs. In a nutshell, if we want to do
something different to get a different result we have to
change our underlying beliefs.

What beliefs do you have about what you do? Write them
down and think about whether a belief you hold could be
flexible.

I believe a good teacher.................................

....

I believe as a teacher I should be....................

....

Good teaching requires...............................

....

Children expect a teacher to be.................

....

Being flexible gives you more options. The person with the most flexibility controls the system.

Beliefs are not the same as values. You could change a belief and still maintain your values about what you do but do it differently.

Some beliefs limit your choices. Make a note of 5 beliefs you hold about teaching the children in your class.

1)

2)

3)

4)

5)

Now look at each one and ask yourself,

'How could I change this belief and do something different to get a different result?'

We're not talking here about changing the fundamental values of a person here. Beliefs change quite organically as we experience different behaviours and results.

Be flexible today and do something differently and note the result. In NLP we talk about the TOTE principle which is

Test – Operate – Test – Exit

This means testing out a different behaviour option, checking the result, test it again and then exit once you have the result you're looking for.

You can't change other people's behaviour but you can change your own to get a different response. You can change your behaviour by changing your beliefs. Some beliefs limit your choices of behaviour and by revisiting them you increase your options to change your behaviour and get the result you want.

2) *You have the resources to do whatever you want*

A core principle of NLP (Neuro Linguistic Programming) is that we already have all the resources we need to do whatever we choose to do.

Over the course of your teaching career and in your private and social life you will have accumulated a huge resource of skills; patience, focus, intuition, clarity, resourcefulness and many others too numerous to itemise.

Sometimes however we trap the skill and categorise it within one of the many roles we play in life. We are inclined to forget that we have that skill already because perhaps we haven't used it enough in our teaching life.

Think about each of the roles you play, the activities you take part in and the social groups you interact with.

Make a list down the left hand side of a piece of paper.

My Role   I am good at   What it means

Now alongside each one, write down what you are good at when you are in that role. Do you make your friends laugh when you are out with them? Are you good at showing people another angle on a problem? Are you a good listener? Make a note of the skills you have in each area of your life.

Now with these two columns complete; look at each of the skills and ask yourself, 'What does that <u>also</u> mean I can do?' write this down in the third column.

For example, I knew a teacher who could do a forward walkover (she used to be a dancer in Pan's People!) which meant that she was flexible in her body and <u>also</u> in her approach to teaching. It is not an automatic assumption but look for how you can take the skill from one area and apply it to another for a positive result.

How can you use this list?

When you are struggling in the classroom or indeed in the staffroom,

- o identify the skill you need
- o think about when and where you had that skill
- o ask yourself, what was the belief you had that enabled you to use that skill

take on that belief now in order to access the skill.

Some people find it easier to do this exercise using a Time Line.

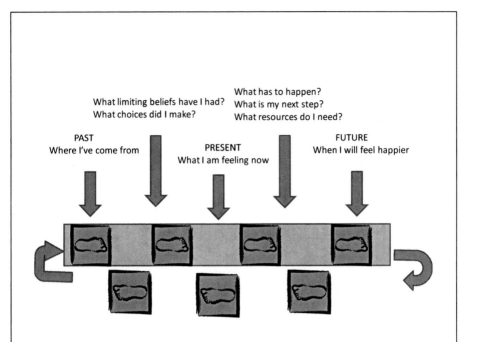

Here is the process.

1) Imagine a line on the floor stretching from the past to the future.

2) Stand on a point that for you represents today.

3) Think about the problem or issue you want to address.

4) Decide on the skills you need to do this effectively.

5) Now look back along the line and identify a point in your past when you demonstrated that particular skill.

6) Stand on that point and recall exactly what you did that demonstrated it most.

7) Anchor it by making an action such as squeezing your earlobe as the memory becomes most vivid. Repeat this a few times to make a strong association.

8) Now return to today's point on the timeline and acknowledge that you do have the skill you need.

9) When you need it in the classroom or staffroom, use your anchor to bring the skill to where you need it now.

You can use the Time Line for many different purposes including goal setting and introduce it to your class to help them access skills and anchor feelings of confidence.

3) If someone else can do it you can too

Have you ever watched someone do something and thought to yourself 'Wow I wish I could do that!'? It could be the way they interact with the class or their computer skills or it could be how they negotiate or gain rapport. Whatever it is – you want it, yes?

Now let me tell you first that the reason you noticed the skill in the other person is because you have it too, otherwise you wouldn't have observed it at all. You may not have the skill to the same extent or perhaps you use that skill somewhere else in your life and don't apply it to your teaching role.

So right now, think of that skill you have noticed in one of your teaching colleagues and write it down. Now look at what you've written because the chances are that what you've written is a bit vague and woolly.

Maybe you've written down 'I like the way Jenny gets all the children involved in her singing class.' That is not precise enough for us to work with. Observe her and notice what exactly she says and does to get that result. Of course you want the result but you first need the underlying belief and the behaviour that it drives.

Watch Jenny's (we call her the model in this situation) body language, how does she use her eyes, her head movements, her arms? Given that she has her back to the class playing the piano she has to make her upper body work. Listen to her tone of voice, pace and volume; how is that having an effect on the class engagement? What about the actual words she uses and the material she has for the class, how is that part of the picture?

You should now have some more precise skills to model to get the result you want. List these and then think about how you already have those skills and how you can model them.

You can practise the movements and the voice at home and you will soon have them as part of your repertoire.

The part you won't have is the underlying belief. That part you need to get from your model.

Find out what your model believes about what they do in the classroom, what is going on in their mind before they take the class and during the class itself. You can tune into that belief and use it instead of the belief you usually use in that situation.

This is also a very powerful classroom exercise because children learn from each other and will realise that they each have something they can model and pass on to their friends. It builds self esteem and mutual respect.

Modelling is a great skill as it means you can be whatever you choose to be and model for others what they want to acquire from you.

There is a chapter on modelling at the end of this book which gives you the process in more detail.

4) *There is no failure only feedback*

Feedback is the nature of the response we get from the class, an individual child, parent, a colleague or the Head. It can be a verbal comment, body language, an email or phone call. The feedback can be directly to you, overheard or passed on to you.

The problem is not the feedback itself; the problem is how we react to it. So how can we as teachers improve the nature of the feedback we give?

One of the best ways is to use 'clean' language free of generalisations, deletions and distortions.

1) Generalisations

Words like *'always', 'never', 'everyone', 'no-one'* are generalisations. They can't possibly be true and there is richer feedback in looking at the exceptions. Focus on the positive and point out that when they did x the result was excellent rather than the many times they did not and the result was disappointing.

Another classic example of a generalisation is *'I can't...'* either verbalised or when the thing they think they 'can't do' is avoided. Some children give up before they start a lesson because they 'can't' do maths. This is a choice we make to 'not be able to do' something. It is the same in self-talk. Have you ever thought 'I can't teach that class' or 'I can't get this child to listen' but *what if you could?*

1) Deletions

We need to give detailed examples so children learn from feedback. Simply saying 'You've worked much better this term' or 'I'm pleased with your progress' deletes the important detail about specifics. When giving feedback, be armed with plenty of precise examples to demonstrate the behaviour you want to focus on and encourage.

2) Distortions

There are three different ways we can distort communication

- Assumptions – when we assume someone else's feelings such as 'You must feel pleased with your test result'. Although it may seem like a reasonable assumption it is more respectful to ask the question. Maybe they were aiming for a higher mark?
- Mind reading – this is predicting the future. An example of this would be saying 'You'll do well in your exams'. Again it is better to ask than mind read.

- Cause and effect – no-one can <u>make</u> you feel a particular way. That is your choice alone. Putting the responsibility for your feelings onto a child or a colleague is a distortion. An example of this would be 'You make me very cross when you talk in the lesson'. Instead own your feelings and say 'I feel very cross when you talk in the lesson because…..' and go on to explain why this is.

Instead of feeling you have failed when you get negative feedback, reframe this with its positive intention which is for you to learn from it.

5) If you try, you won't succeed

How many times a day do we ask children to 'try' to do something? We remember perhaps our own parents urging us to 'just try your best'. Yet there is built-in failure in the word 'try'. Notice when you use this word and reword your sentence without the word 'try' so children will be more motivated. 'Try' presupposes they will find it difficult so they are expecting to give up on the exercise more quickly than if your expectation was that they could do it.

Imagine there are two boxes in front of you and I ask you to pick up the first one. You will pick it up quite easily because you assume it must be light.

Now I ask you to 'try' and pick up the other. Immediately you expect the other box to be heavier and you may have difficulty picking it up. If I then said, 'try hard' or 'just try it', I am emphasising the difficulty and you may look at it wondering how heavy it is and even consider asking for help. In fact the boxes are the same weight. The only difference is our expectations of how heavy the second box is.

You will sometimes be presenting harder exercises and children may find them difficult so present the exercise as something they can do rather than something they can't do and will need to 'try'. There is an element of struggle about the word 'try' which is not enabling in a teaching environment. Just ask them to 'do it'.

When children in your class respond with the word 'try' such as 'Well I'll try and do it' or if you ask them to behave and they say 'I'll try'. Your resourceful and encouraging response is 'You know you can do it'.

I asked a child recently what his goal was for the new term. He said *'I'm going to try not to get into trouble this term'.* This is not going to work.

Firstly, using the word 'try' means he already expects to get into trouble so it won't be long before he does.

Secondly, his goal is an 'away from' goal in that he is aiming for avoiding something rather than having a positive 'towards goal' of achieving something.

Thirdly, he is focussing on what he doesn't want rather than what he does want. What you focus on is generally what you get.

Do you use the word 'try' in your self-talk? Do you 'try' to teach a difficult class or 'try' to get on with a demanding parent or 'try' to explain a maths principle simply?

There is built-in failure in the word 'try'. Just 'do it'.

6) The map is not the territory

We experience the world through our five senses; sight, hearing, touch, smell and taste. Two million bits of information bombard our unconscious mind yet our conscious mind can only cope with about 7. So how do we get from 2 million down to 7? What we do is filter the inputs.

How we filter them will depend on our beliefs and values, what is important to us individually and where we put our attention. Our filter will also be determined by our life experiences, our social and cultural background and in this context, our teaching experience.

So you can imagine that for each one of us, the 7 bits of information that form our own map will reflect the territory (the 2 million available bits of information) very differently. Your map will be very different from that of the children in your class but their maps will probably be fairly similar to each other which is why when they all laugh at something they find funny in the lesson, you feel excluded.

If you've had years of teaching the same year group you probably have a very good insight into their map but if you haven't and you're teaching a new year group this term, enter their territory by stepping into their shoes and seeing it from their viewpoint.

Use metaphors to increase your understanding of their map. As you know, a metaphor is when we describe the problem situation in terms of an unrelated experience and by so doing, see the situation in a different light that enables us to have clarity.

Here's an example of how to use clean questions and metaphors.

Teacher: What's learning French like?

Child: It's confusing like when you get lost in the supermarket for a moment and wonder where your mum is.

Teacher: Confusing, like getting lost in the supermarket?

Child: Yes like you don't know which aisle to go down.

Teacher: You don't know which aisle to go down?

Child: Well you could go down one but it could be wrong and you'd get more lost.

Teacher: It could be wrong and you could get more lost?

Child: So you just stand still and hope your mum comes back for you because it's less scary to do nothing.

Teacher: You hope your mum comes back for you?

Child: Or someone to tell me where my mum is.

Using the metaphor you have a great insight into how this child's map works and why she doesn't answer questions in your French lesson. What she needs are some signposts. She needs to feel safe and have some options. Not doing anything seems safer because she wants you to give her the answer and she won't risk being further confused by giving the wrong one.

She needs to know that one of the answers in her head (aisles) is the right one and that if she thinks hard she may remember what you told her about that grammar rule (her mother said she had to buy) and get the answer right (find her in that aisle).How pleased she would be and how much more confident.

How you see the world is different from how others see it. Enter their territory by stepping into their shoes and seeing it from their viewpoint.

Parents have a different map as well, as do teachers with different responsibilities. Spend time to understand their map to build rapport.

7) *Look for the pay off and the positive intention*

Assume everyone has a positive intention and be curious about it. Even behaviour that seems outrageous and disruptive, self-sabotaging and aggressive is giving your student some bizarre positive pay off and it is our challenge as teachers to find out what this may be because the negative behaviour won't stop until the positive intention is recognised and satisfied.

Our job is to find out what the positive intention is behind the bad behaviour and seek out with the student a way of satisfying the positive intention in a positive rather than a negative way.

We do things for a reason. If we see behaviour we don't want, consider how your students can get the pay off they seek without the behaviour.

Let me introduce you to the NLP parts integration tool that you can use with your students.

Exercise

Hold out your right hand and imagine that on it is a person who holds one of the values that you feel strongly about. Imagine the value, how you are manifesting it and all the aspects of it that are on your mind.

Now hold out the other hand and imagine that on this hand is another person who holds a different value or option. Again, build it up with all the aspects you have under consideration.

With both hands held outstretched in front of you, look at each of them in turn and ask person A (your right hand) what it wants for you, what is its positive intent? Now do the same to person B on your left hand.

Are there common elements? Could the two 'people' agree a common goal and means of achieving it?

Continue getting these two parts of you to offer solutions around the common positive goal until you feel you have a resolution.

Before you finish just check in with both parts that by agreeing there are no negative repercussions as a result of one part not doing what it wanted to do, that will prove problematic.

This technique is great for dealing with internal conflict such as choosing between two equally appealing or unwanted options.

You can introduce it to children as a way of getting them to consider alternative behaviour by offering them the ability to still meet the positive intention of the unwanted behaviour.

8) *Mind the gap*

Before responding, stop and consider how an impartial bystander might see or hear the situation differently. This is called 'disassociating' and by doing this we allow time to enter the other person's map and work out their positive intention and pay off.

Responding spontaneously tends to come from our own map and be a more emotional personal response, inappropriately defensive.

This next section covers some very hands on NLP tools and techniques to learn and add to your teaching skills.

1. Selling the 'sizzle'

2. VAK

3. Self Esteem

4. Feedback

5. Modelling

6. State Management

WORKSHEET 1: SELLING THE SIZZLE

As teachers we have lesson plans and they tend to reflect the curriculum needs as well as incorporating the children's interests, topical events and our own ideas.

There's a lot to get through so how do we get 'buy in'?

The best way to get the class behind you is to tell them what they will be able to do by the end of the class, how they can use this new skill and how they will feel about knowing it. We need to talk about the benefits, what they will get from the lesson and how they can use the skill or the information in their everyday lives.

We can use quotes and stories to convey the sizzle by recounting a story of a child who having learnt this was able to apply it in some interesting or amusing way. 'I bumped into someone I taught last year and she was saying how she remembered this lesson when she was helping her mum with the shopping and she noticed they were given the wrong change. Her mum was so pleased she gave her the £1 difference'.

Use metaphors to sell the sizzle for example ' knowing how to do x is like knowing all the cheats in x (pick a PlayStation or Wii game they all play)' or if they are football mad 'you'll feel like you've scored a hat trick once you've got the hang of this'.

Then we need to hook them into the lesson activity and we can do this in various ways but the embedded command can be very effective.

Embedded commands

In NLP terms an embedded command is when you embed or place the direction to the class within a sentence such that it becomes a hypnotic phrase that they absorb subconsciously. We do this with the 'sizzle'.

Here is the structure of the embedded command

1) Start with a phrase like
   a. When you
   b. As you
   c. You might find that
   d. How surprised would you be to
   e. What would it be like if
2) Pause
3) Then the command verb for what you want the children to do such as listen, work, write, read etc
4) Pause
5) Desirable outcome or state such as being able to do the maths, answer the question etc
6) Tag such as 'will you?' with a downward inflection not used as a question in other words but as a command.

Here are some examples:

- You might find that (pause) when you answer the questions (pause) you will know some very interesting facts about the Vikings, don't you think?

- What would it be like if you (pause) worked through your times tables quickly without talking (pause) and then we'll feel we've worked really well today, won't we?

- As you (pause) do this experiment following the instructions on the sheet (pause) you will see how the leaf takes on the colour through the veins, won't you?

Tag questions tend to invite agreement and can also be used throughout the lesson to reinforce the desirable outcome and the state by saying 'you're enjoying this, aren't you?' or 'you're finding this interesting, aren't you?' or 'you're finding this easy aren't you?'

Focus on what you **do** want

Another aspect of embedded commands also relates to how we process information.

If someone were to say 'Don't think about pink elephants!' you immediately create an image of a pink elephant in your mind because how could you 'not think' about them without doing that?

It's the same with children. We need to be clear at the start of the lesson, what we <u>do</u> want and focus on that, giving feedback appropriately (see Worksheet 2). For example, 'I want you all to listen to me for a few minutes and then I have some worksheets to do. When we finish them quickly, we'll have time for a quick game before the end of the lesson.'

The word *'try'*

This word has failure embedded in it. It presupposes you will find something difficult. If someone asks you to try and do an exercise then you wonder if you will be able to do it. If they ask you to 'really try' or 'please try' it now sounds even harder. There is an element of struggle about the word 'try' which is not enabling in a teaching environment.

The word *'but'*

Whatever you say before will be negated by the 'but' word and everything after it is emphasised. For example, 'I know this is hard but you're all doing so well' will emphasise how well they are doing and minimise how hard the exercise may be. Had you said it the other way round 'You're all doing so well but I know the exercise is hard' some children would decide that indeed it was hard and may give up.

The word 'if'

This indicates that there is a choice available so if there isn't, use a different word such as 'and'.

WORKSHEET 2: VAK

Many schools use VAK already so you may well be
familiar with the concept but for those who aren't, this
worksheet will give you the basic concept and some ideas
about how to implement the learnings into your teaching
style.

VAK refers to the three ways in which we communicate;
visually, auditory and kinaesthetic. Although we use all
three, we tend to have a preferred one and children are
less adept than adults at switching between them in order
to maximise their understanding so it is particularly
important for teachers to be able to recognise which a
student prefers so they can adjust their way of
communicating their message.

In a classroom with a number of children with different
VAKs you need to present information in all three styles to
cover everyone's preference.

Visual

Some children prefer to see the information written on a board or white screen, on a worksheet or in a book. They have a vivid visual imagination and notice and absorb what they see better than what they hear. If you see a child apparently day dreaming they may be putting images to what they hear by accessing their visual memory. Mind maps are a good way for them to gather information.

Show them pictures, words and ideas rather than tell them. They tend to link words with images. They also read better with illustrations that correspond with the text and will be better at writing sums than mental arithmetic. When doing sums in their head they will picture the sum as if it is written on a page and mentally visualise themselves doing the sum in order to get the correct answer.

When you communicate with a visual child ask questions like 'Can you see that?' or 'Do you see how we do that?'Draw their attention by asking them to 'Look at this' and 'Let me show you how to do this'.

Auditory

Children who have an auditory preference like to talk and hear information and will remember the sounds of words spoken and pay more attention to how they sound rather than what they look like.

They will pay close attention to what you say and may prefer to read aloud and do their sums out loud rather than silently. They will work better in pairs with auditory preferenced children working together so they can discuss the work.

Auditory children get easily distracted by noise so may get upset in a very noisy environment.

They usually love music and have a good ear for singing and playing instruments. Use songs and rhythm such as drumming for learning times tables or facts that they need to remember. Mnemonics also work well for revising for tests.

When you communicate with an auditory child ask them ' Can you understand what I'm saying', 'Listen to me', 'Let's talk about...' and 'How does this sound to you?'

Kinaesthetic

Kinaesthetic children can be quite fidgety and want to be actively doing things rather than watching and listening.

They learn best by activity so using counting beads, Cuisenaire rods, sandpaper letters and numbers and other physical or interactive learning materials suit them best.

You will find them wanting to use the computer so they can physically learn rather than reading books or doing sums.

As well as being physically active they will also tend to touch other children more, hug them or hit them, want to sit very close to them and be unaware when they are invading another child's space.

They express themselves best with body language and facial expressions and may not contribute much in class or appear to be working hard so they need to be asked directly if you notice them looking uncomfortable or confused.

Communicate with them by asking 'Do you get this?', 'Can you do this?', 'Show me how to...' and 'Shall we work through this together?'

How it works in practice

In the classroom it helps to put similar children together as this will be more effective than combining ability because you can then use their preferred communication when explaining to that table rather than using all three styles for the whole class.

You can also give them more appropriate tasks and exercises for the class topic that will suit their preference and when each table contributes the rest of the class will get the benefit of three ways of approaching the same topic.

Encourage them to understand how different types of approach work and how to recognise them because as they get older they will need to be more flexible.

Be aware of your own preference and remember that by simply offering one communication style you are making it hard to understand your lesson for about two thirds of the class. Materials need to have three dimensions to cover all the children.

The schools who have introduced NLP effectively into their teaching have sent information out to parents explaining what they are doing, how to recognise which preference their child has and explanations of how to help them with their homework using NLP.

In Worksheet 4 we will look at feedback and of course this needs to be given in the preference of the child for it to have maximum effect.

WORKSHEET 3: SELF ESTEEM

We all suffer from low self esteem at some time or the other, don't we? There will always be children in your class who suffer from low self esteem.

There could be several reasons for lack of self esteem.

1) Limiting beliefs

These are beliefs about ourselves that limit our choice of behaviour. For example, if a child is 'labelled' at home as 'the naughty child' or 'the stupid child' or even 'the clever child', they may feel compelled even if subconsciously to live up (or down) to that identity.

Children following a sibling through the school will tend to feel compared to their older sibling despite the teachers' attempts not to do so. If their older sibling was very clever, very sporty or musical, younger children will lack self esteem even if they have just as strong talents in other areas.

We are given limiting beliefs at school, from parents and carers at home and other significant people in our life. As children we believe what we are told when we are young and carry (possibly) these false beliefs into teenage and adult life.

It can be quite difficult to challenge a limiting belief because they can be self fulfilling. For example a child might have been told that he is useless at maths (possibly by another child, an older sibling or a parent) and therefore doesn't really listen to you explaining how to do the particular maths exercise. The child then gets it wrong and this confirms his belief that he is useless. If in fact we ask the child to pretend or 'act as if' he is a maths genius he would probably get the exercise correct.

2) We are externally referenced

If we constantly compare ourselves with others, particularly those who we think are cleverer, better looking or more popular than us, we suffer from self esteem.

The answer is to 'disassociate' which means to see ourselves as others see us. Write down or tell yourself how you think your friends would describe you. Pretending to be someone else enables you to view yourself more favourably and notice what others notice. When you do this with children, prompt them by commenting on things you have noticed or that other teachers have commented on.

Use an exercise called 'perceptual positioning' to help with this.

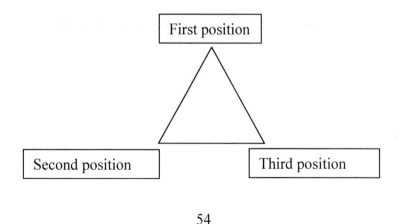

Put out three chairs and explain that one is 'first position' (I) one is second position (you) and the other is third position (they).

Ask them to sit in first position and encourage them to talk about how they feel about themselves, what doesn't seem to be working and how frustrated they feel. Resist the temptation to sympathise or contradict and allow them to do the exercise themselves.

They then sit in second position and pretend they are the person they envy or feel inspired by, someone they feel less confident than. As that person they talk to first position (themselves) about what they think of them.

They go back to first position and respond. You can allow them to switch chairs as often as they need to to have this exchange. They can choose the other chair to be their teacher if this helps and the teacher is the person they are having problems with. If this is the case it is obviously advisable for a different teacher to oversee the perceptual positioning exercise.

When all's been said, the child sits in position three and comments on all they've heard as an impartial observer.

Finally, the child returns to position one and responds as himself again as to what he feels is his best way forward now he's heard all the other views.

This exercise usually results in children acknowledging their own strengths as seen by others.

Use this exercise yourself to challenge your own limiting beliefs.

3) Our goals may be unrealistic

We sometimes set goals that are not within our control or within their reach. This may have been prompted by expectations from home or perhaps they aspire to be another Wayne Rooney! Constantly striving for something out of their grasp can be dispiriting so use the NLP goal setting principles.

a) First and foremost goals need to be POSITIVE

Encourage your students to word their goals as 'towards goals' what they want to achieve rather than what they want to avoid. What do they want? It needs to be specific too so what mark do they want in the test or what book would they like to be able to read, what level book? What level maths book do they want to be on? Which times table do they want to know well?

b) How will they recognise when they have achieved it? What EVIDENCE do they need to have that have achieved their goal?

This could be that they show they have achieved the level or goal in a test or their report at the end of the term. Maybe they want to have the confidence to speak up in class or perform in a school play? What will other children and you their teacher see or hear them do that will demonstrate that they have achieved their goal?

c) When and where do they want to have this resource? What is the CONTEXT?

Ask children to think about which lessons they need to focus on and what skills they need to achieve this goal. Where do they already have the skills? Perhaps they need focus to achieve it or concentration. Where have you seen them demonstrate this skill, perhaps in another lesson, in PE or music or in the playground? How can they apply this skill to the context they need it in to achieve their goal?

d) The goal needs to be SELF ACHIEVABLE. They need to have the ability to achieve the goal themselves.

They cannot have a goal that relies on others. For example, they have no control over getting the top mark in a test because it relies on others to get lower marks than them. They also cannot have a goal to win a race for the same reason.

Arguably they will be relying on you for support in achieving their goal but ultimately it will be their work and commitment to the goal that will ensure they achieve it.

e) What will be the ADVANTAGES AND DISADVANTAGES of achieving it?

Whilst the advantages of achieving their goal will be obvious in terms of enhanced self esteem, sometimes the disadvantages are less obvious. Children sometimes get labelled 'geeks' by others in the class when they do well and they may separate themselves from their peers by getting higher marks or becoming more confident. How can they still achieve their goal whilst avoiding the disadvantages that could sabotage their efforts?

f) What is the BENEFIT of this outcome?

By achieving their goal, what benefit will they obtain? What will become available to them that was not before? What values do they have in life that will be met by achieving their goal? How worthwhile will it be? What negative feeling will they no longer have?

4) Their goals may be 'away from' goals

If children focus on what they don't want such as aiming 'not to fail an important exam' or 'not to get kicked out of school' they are putting their energy into something negative which will not help build self esteem. Instead encourage them to set 'towards' goals that are worded in the positive and are what they want, not what they don't want.

5) They don't recognise their skills

Similarly children who focus on what they can't do are putting their attention on something negative and would have more self esteem if they focussed on what they can do. Remind them what they are good at and suggest they keep a diary and note each day 10 things that they did well. These can be seemingly small things like picking up a piece of litter and putting it in the bin through to getting good marks or playing nicely with someone in the playground.

6) They are not in rapport

Being in rapport with those around them is about matching the behaviour, body language and VAK of those they interact with.

Some children have a 'mismatch' pattern and want to be different because they want to be noticed. They make a point of doing something different from their peers or what is expected of them. Whilst they will be in trouble, it gives them the attention they seek. Look at ways they can achieve their pay off without the behaviour. Offer them other ways to get attention through taking responsibility or leading a project. Ask them who they admire among their peers.

Character or personality traits they have observed in others will be present in them too; that's how they have been aware of them. Show them how you have noticed this trait in them and encourage them to display this more often and notice when they do.

Here is a game you can play with any age children and it works really well in getting them to think about their skills and build self esteem.

- Place two rows of chairs (call one row A and one row B)facing each other in a row so everyone has a chair and ask everyone to sit down facing someone.

- Row A tell their opposite in row B about a person who inspires them, a celebrity, famous sportsperson, political leader etc They give 3 reasons and the person in row B is not allowed to say anything.

- Row A moves one place on and Row B does the talking and row A stays silent.

- Row A moves on one more and tells row B opposite how they inspire others and again row B says nothing.

- Row A moves one place on and row B does the talking with row A saying nothing.

WORKSHEET 4: FEEDBACK

An important belief that underpins NLP is that there is no failure only feedback. Yet how often do children at school feel they have failed? How often do we as teachers feel we have failed?

Feedback is the nature of the response we get from the class, an individual child, parent, a colleague or the Head. It can be a verbal comment, body language, an email or phone call. The feedback can be directly to you, overheard or passed on to you. The problem is not the feedback itself; the problem is how we react to it.

According to NLP, we must look for the positive intention. The positive intention of feedback is that we can learn from it and do something different next time we are in that situation. After all if we always do what we've always done we will always get what we've always got. We cannot change other people's behaviour but we can change our own.

We also give feedback as teachers, don't we? Given that we want to focus on the positive intention ourselves, how can we give feedback in a way that others will learn from it?

One of the best ways of learning from feedback is to challenge 'dirty' language so let's examine the forms that can take.

There are 3 and they describe ways we sometimes 'dirty' communication so it becomes difficult to learn from.

1) Generalisations

These are when we suggest in our feedback that someone 'always' or 'never' does something, when 'everyone else does/knows'. This can't possibly be true and there is richer feedback in looking at the exceptions. For example, focus on the positive and point out that when they did x the result was excellent rather than the many times they did not and the result was unsatisfactory.

A classic example of a generalisation is 'I can't...' either verbalised or when the thing they think they 'can't do' is avoided. Some children give up before they start a lesson 'can't' do maths. This is a choice we make to not be able to do something. You may be in the situation where you are telling someone 'I can't teach that class' or 'I can't get this child to listen' but what if you could?

2) Deletions

In order for feedback to be helpful we need to give detailed examples so they can learn from it. Simply saying 'You've worked much better this term' or 'I'm pleased with your progress' deletes the important detail about specifics. When giving feedback be armed with plenty of precise examples to demonstrate the behaviour you want to focus on and encourage.

3) Distortions

There are three different ways we can distort communication

- Assumptions – when we assume someone else's feelings such as 'You must feel pleased with your test result'. You don't know this and it may seem like a reasonable assumption but it will be more respectful to ask the question than assume the answer.

- Mind reading – similarly predicting the future can be unhelpful in a feedback scenario. An example of this would be saying 'You'll do well in your exams'. That may well be what you think but it may not be their expectation at all. Again it is better to ask than mind read.

- Cause and effect – no-one can make you feel a particular way. That is your choice alone. Putting the responsibility for your feelings onto a child or a colleague is also a distortion. An example of this would be 'You make me very cross when you talk in the lesson'. It would be more respectful to simply own your own feelings and say 'I feel very cross when you talk in the lesson because.....' and go on to explain why this is.

Some feedback, however positively reframed, is still not welcome possibly because we think it is unjustified. If that is the case the first thing to do is 'disassociate'.

This is an NLP technique which calls us to imagine we are an impartial witness, maybe another teacher in school. Would they give you the same feedback? If so, act on it and behave differently. If you want a different result it is you who has to change.

Maybe it isn't the case and the feedback is indeed unjustified. Rather than take it personally, which we often do, take the opportunity to present your case with detailed examples and challenge the feedback..........in rapport.

In our working lives, as in our home life, rapport is essential to smooth and 'clean' communication, without distortions, deletions and generalisations and using the VAK preference of the other person.

Truly 'clean language' can be achieved by reflecting the language of the other person and using metaphors to gain clearer understanding without putting your own 'stuff' in. For example, 'what is it like for you in a maths class?' or 'what's it been like being in this class?'

Metaphors allow us to use our own images and feelings and provide much richer communication than just words and work extremely well across cultures as they transcend boundaries.

As teachers we experience feedback from parents about their children and we have to give feedback to them at parents' evenings and in reports. Use these principles to give feedback in the way we would like to receive it. Use the 'sandwich' approach by emphasising the positive first, giving detailed examples. Then offer areas for improvement and finish on a positive note.

WORKSHEET 5: MODELLING

What is it?

The unique feature of NLP is modelling. Modelling is the copying of a skill you observe in someone else that you want for yourself. The 'model' is the person or child who has the skill that is wanted. They should be an excellent example of that skill. The 'modeller' is the person who wants to add that skill to their repertoire. It is a fantastic opportunity for you as a teacher to learn from your colleagues and for children to learn from each other.

How do we know what we need or want to model? Let's suppose we are having difficulty doing something, say controlling a class or explaining a difficult concept in a lesson.

- Identify the skill we need. Is it patience or clarity of speech, knowledge, authoritative tone of voice? Be specific about what you need or discuss with the student what they think they need

- Now be observant and seek out people who have that skill and ask them if you can model it. Most people are very flattered to be asked and want to help. They might even ask if they can model a skill you have.

- Choose a few models because some people are better able than others to help you and the more models you have of the skill, the better you will be able to copy it.

- In order to acquire the skill you will also need to understand the model's underlying belief that enables them to do what they do because if you had that belief, you too would be able to do it. You need to take on the same belief therefore.

For example, in order to control a lively class the model has to believe she or he has the skills in the first place. You have the skills too but not the belief which is why you want to model them.

Here is the Modelling process:

- Observe the structure, how they do it step by step
- Ask them what they believe about their skill
- What is going on in their head just before they do it
- Imagine you have that belief
- Practise it until you have that belief as well
- Incorporate it into your repertoire of skills

A skill can be as small as simply a facial expression or gesture, a sports skill, teaching skill, anything that you admire in someone else. Be curious about the skill and notice every aspect of it. Look at when they do it, how they do it and what comes first, second third and so on. Maybe someone on TV or in a movie has this skill you can use them as a model but you won't get the underlying belief from them.

Identify the exact nature of the skill. It's much easier to model something specific rather than something vague. For example you might admire the way someone 'teaches a class' or a child might admire another child who 'has lots of friends' but that is too vague and there are many skills involved in each of these.

You need to break down what you have observed into small parts and identify exactly what these are.

Find examples of excellence for that precise skill. It could be that those who do that particular skill with excellence don't use it in the way you intend to use it but for the purposes of modelling this doesn't matter. Spend time watching those with the skill and note down everything you observe. Practise whenever you can and be curious about the response you get. Is it starting to work?

Some of your models will be easier to approach than others but with those who you feel confident with, ask them how they do the thing you are observing. You can be specific, 'I've noticed how you are very good at getting x to take the minutes at the meeting, how do you do that?'
It is not unusual for people not to know how they do something they do well because they do it quite naturally and possibly have been doing it for years.
You need to dig deeper and ask about their underlying beliefs. If we use the analogy of the potter it may help explain why this is important.

If you are watching a potter mould a lump of clay you can guess what he is making and you can copy what he does but you will only make the same thing as the potter if you know what the potter is imaging in his head about what form the clay will take.

It can seem intrusive in a work context so you may need to do this with models of the skill whom you know well outside work. Ask 'I've noticed how you are very good at getting x to eat foods he doesn't like. What belief do you have about your ability to get him to do this?'Here we have found the skill in our personal life and a model who you can ask about underlying beliefs. The structure is about getting a child to do something they don't want to do and you can apply this in your teaching role.

Once you have the underlying belief or indeed several from different models, match their belief about this skill with your own. You need to acquire the belief. First you need to examine your belief and where it comes from. Maybe it is from childhood and no longer useful to you in your current environment or in the workplace.

When parents pass on beliefs to children they are not necessarily thinking that they will apply them in a work environment.

Beliefs are not values, they can be changed as we gather new information and experiences. Re-examine your limiting beliefs because it is restricting your options. You can model any skill you want whether that be in a sports and fitness situation, personally or work related. Once you have the structure and the belief you have the skill.

In a work context you can use NLP modelling for team building and career development by explaining the process and asking them which skills they'd like to model in other team members. By doing this you create an enabling environment rich in new language and greater awareness of each other's gifts and overall you will grow the team's capabilities and trust.

Use this space to write down what skills you've observed in your colleagues that you'd like to have for yourself.

I want this skill   *From*

Now write down below what you could pass on to them.

This is a very powerful exercise in a classroom situation because children can learn from each other and realise that they each have something they can model and pass on to their friends. It builds self esteem and mutual respect.

Modelling is a great skill as it means you can be whatever you choose to be and model for others what they want to acquire from you. Apply it to every part of your life as ongoing personal development.

WORKSHEET 6: STATE MANAGEMENT

Just as you can tell when one of the children in your class is in a bad mood, so can they pick up cues about your mood. What you bring into the classroom with you will be conveyed to your class in seconds. You cannot 'not communicate'. We convey our state by the way we stand or sit, how we hold our head and how we walk into the classroom before you've even said a word.

If you sense that your state is not resourceful here's a quick way to change it. We can do this using the SWISH technique from our NLP toolbox.

1) First we need to find out what the trigger factor is. What prompts the negative response? Is it something someone says such as 'Double maths this morning' or 'Ofsted inspection next week' or something seen such as the word 'Test' on the board or someone texting under their desk. Is it something felt such as overexcitement in the classroom or it could just be very hot?

Identify the unwanted behaviour or response and the trigger.

What pay off is there for the response? What is the positive intention?

In NLP we know that there is always a positive intention and it is our challenge to find it.

Perhaps the unwanted response delays the start of the lesson or causes laughter in the classroom?

2) Now ask yourself what the desired response would be to the trigger. What would be the desired behaviour? Will they still be able to meet their positive intention or another different positive intention using the new response? Ask them to get an image in their mind of them doing the desired behaviour. What will they look like, sound like and feel like?

3) Check for the ecology. Are there any pitfalls or disadvantages of the desired behaviour?

4) Now ask them to imagine doing the usual unwanted behaviour and picture it like a film with Hollywood effects, the colour, actors, music and great sound. They are not in the picture, they can choose an actor to play them in their imagination.

5) The next step is to put the image of the new behaviour in the bottom left hand corner of the screen as you might if you're checking what's on another TV channel. This time they are in the picture as themself.

6) Then they say 'SWISH' and at that moment they bring their hand across their face as if swatting away a fly. Switch the images so the new behaviour is the big frame with the unwanted behaviour very small in the corner.

7) Repeat the steps a few times until they can do this quickly and easily and can use it whenever they need to replace unwanted behaviours or responses.

Use this yourself for your own unwanted responses as well! Once you get practised at this, you will have a great anchor for your desired state.

AND FINALLY

If there is anything you are unsure about or would like to work on, please get in touch with me judy@engagingnlp.com or via my website www.engagingnlp.com and I would be happy to explain further or arrange an NLP coaching session in your school either with your teachers or children.

Bibliography

NLP at work	Sue Knight	Nicholas Brealey
Happy Kids Happy You	Sue Beever	Crown House
Brilliant Parent	Emma Sargent	Prentice Hall
The complete secrets of happy children	Steve & Sharon Biddulph	Thorsons
Connecting with your teen	John P Oda	Booklocker.com
How to talk so kids will listen and listen so kids will talk	Adele Faber & Elaine Mazlish	Simon & Schuster
Teach yourself NLP	Steve Bavister & Amanda Vickers	Hodder
Teach yourself Bringing up happy children	Glenda Weil & Doro Marden	Hodder
NLP for Teachers Publishing	Richard Churches and Roger Terry	Crown House
TA for teens	Alvyn M Freed	Jalmar Press
The Satir Model	Virginia Satir	Science and Behaviour
Think Good Feel Good	Paul Stallard	Wiley

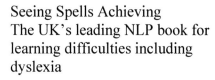

Seeing Spells Achieving
The UK's leading NLP book for
learning difficulties including
dyslexia

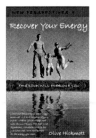

Stop Bedwetting in 7 Days
A simple step-by-step guide to help
children conquer bedwetting
problems in just a few days

Recover Your Energy
NLP for Chronic Fatigue, ME and
tiredness

More NLP books at www.mxpublishing.co.uk

Play Magic Golf
How to use self-hypnosis,
meditation, Zen, universal laws,
quantum energy, and the latest
psychological and NLP techniques
to be a better golfer

Psychobabble
A straight forward, plain English
guide to the benefits of NLP

You Too Can Do Health
Improve Your Health and
Wellbeing, Through the Inspiration
of One Person's Journey of Self-
development and Self-awareness
Using NLP, energy and the Secret
Law of Attraction

Process and Prosper
Inspiring and motivational book
from necrotising faciitis survivor
Wendy Harrington. Amazing book
for anyone facing critical trauma.

Bangers and Mash
Battling throat cancer with the help
of an NLP coach. Keith's story has
led to changes in procedure in
many cancer hospitals and is an
inspiration to cancer patients
everywhere.

Performance Strategies for
Musicians
Tackle stage fright and
performance anxiety using NLP.